DENALI

National Park and Preserve

(FORMERLY MOUNT MCKINLEY NATIONAL PARK)

by Ruth Radlauer

Photographs by Rick McIntyre
Ed and Ruth Radlauer

AN ELK GROVE BOOK

 CHILDRENS PRESS, CHICAGO

For authentication of the manuscript and maps, the author is grateful to National Park personnel and members of the Alaska Natural History Association.

Photo Credits:
Rick McIntyre: Cover and pages 13, 15, 21 (bull moose)
23 (arctic ground squirrels)
25 (ptarmigan), 27, 29, 31, 33 (lamb),
35, 37 (wolf),
39 (fox, caribou, vole), 45
National Park Service, page 23 (bearberry)

Artifacts page 41 courtesy of Nedra Fox

Cover: Mount McKinley And Caribou

Library of Congress Cataloging in Publication Data

Radlauer, Ruth Shaw.
  Denali National Park and Preserve (formerly Mt. McKinley National Park)

  (Parks for people)
  "An Elk Grove book."
  Summary: Presents the geography, plant and animal
life, and distinctive features of this national park
located in an area south of the Arctic Circle.
  1. Denali National Park and Preserve (Alaska)—
Juvenile literature.   [1. Denali National Park and
Preserve (Alaska)   2. National parks and reserves]
I. McIntyre, Rick.   II. Radlauer, Ed.   III. Title.
IV. Series.
F912.M23R32   917.98'3   81-3876

1 2 3 4 5 6 7 8 9 10 11 12 13 14 15 R 87 86 85 84 83 82 81

Contents

What is Denali National Park and Preserve ?

Denali National Park is discovery. In this park you may find the last frontier of America. Here, in this Alaskan wilderness, are huge areas untouched by human feet.

This is a land where winters are long and cold. But during the long days of June and July, the sun hardly sets.

At Denali, you'll discover satin-smooth lakes and zebra-striped mountains. This park is the rushing of rivers, the silence of a forest, and the bark of sled dogs eager to run. It's the spring of your step on a soft forest floor and the nip of wind that almost whisks you away.

Here you'll discover BIG. The highest mountain in the U.S., Mount McKinley, pokes its snowy peaks into the clouds. If the clouds lift, you feel small beside this monster mountain.

At Denali, you may even discover yourself. How far can you hike? How many animals can you see as you ride through the park on a shuttle bus? How many tundra plants can you recognize after a Discovery Hike? And how do you fit into this wild world of Denali National Park and Preserve?

page 4

ou Can Go By Train

Some Mountains Look Zebra-Striped

warf Rhododendron

Residents—Grizzly Sow And Cubs

Your Trip to Denali National Park

A trip to Denali National Park begins when your family flies or drives to Anchorage or Fairbanks, Alaska. From these cities, Alaska Highway 3 takes you to the park, or you can take the train. From Anchorage, a train ride means eight hours of travel through fantastic scenery. A train trip from Fairbanks takes half as long.

Except to reach a campsite, private cars are not allowed inside the park beyond the Savage River Bridge. A free shuttle bus will take you anywhere along the gravel road that goes through the park to Wonder Lake. You can camp in one of seven campgrounds or stay at hotels near the entrance.

Winter or summer, you need to be prepared for freezing weather as well as warm days. Your packing list should include layers of sweaters and a jacket, wool socks and cap, rain gear, hiking boots, a water bottle, and day pack or backpack. Binoculars are wonderful, but you can see lots of wildlife without them.

For a map and list of park books and pamphlets, write the Superintendent, Denali National Park and Preserve, P.O. Box 9, McKinley Park, Alaska 99755.

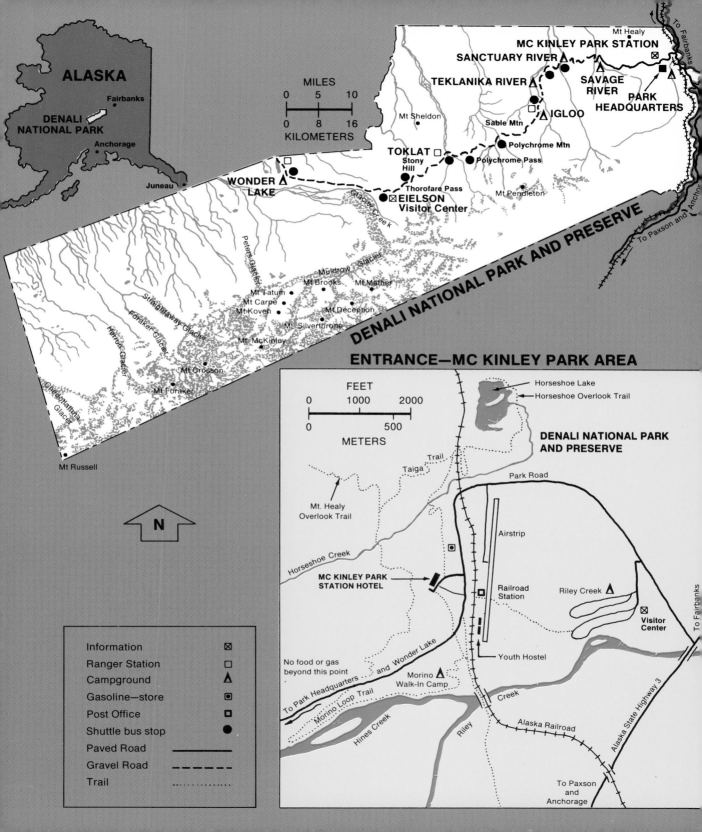

ALASKA

Fairbanks

DENALI
NATIONAL PARK

Anchorage

Juneau

MILES
0   5   10

0   8   16
KILOMETERS

Mt Healy

MC KINLEY PARK STATION
SANCTUARY RIVER
TEKLANIKA RIVER
Mt Sheldon
Sable Mtn
SAVAGE RIVER
PARK HEADQUARTERS
IGLOO
To Fairbanks

Polychrome Mtn
Polychrome Pass
TOKLAT
Stony Hill
Thorofare Pass
Mt Pendleton
WONDER LAKE
Glacier Creek
EIELSON Visitor Center

To Paxson and Anchor

DENALI NATIONAL PARK AND PRESERVE

Peters Glacier
Muldrow Glacier
Mt Brooks
Mt Mather
Mt Tatum
Mt Carpe
Mt Koven
Mt Deception
Straightaway Glacier
Foraker Glacier
Mt Silverthrone
Mt McKinley
Harper Glacier
Mt Crosson
Mt Foraker
Okonohatana Glacier
Mt Russell

N

ENTRANCE—MC KINLEY PARK AREA

FEET
0   1000   2000

0   500
METERS

Horseshoe Lake
Horseshoe Overlook Trail

DENALI NATIONAL PARK AND PRESERVE

Trail
Taiga
Park Road
Mt. Healy Overlook Trail
Airstrip
Horseshoe Creek
MC KINLEY PARK STATION HOTEL
Railroad Station
Riley Creek
Visitor Center
To Fairbanks
Youth Hostel
No food or gas beyond this point
and Wonder Lake
To Park Headquarters
Morino Loop Trail
Morino Walk-In Camp
Creek
Hines Creek
Riley
Alaska Railroad
Alaska State Highway 3
To Paxson and Anchorage

Legend

Information	⊠
Ranger Station	☐
Campground	⛺
Gasoline—store	⊙
Post Office	⊡
Shuttle bus stop	●
Paved Road	——
Gravel Road	-- -- --
Trail	·········

Besides warm clothes, the most important things to take to Denali are your five senses. You also need a mind that wants to know and a wish to discover Alaska.

You'll bring more understanding with you if you read some books about the park and its wild residents. Add to these a word list, and you'll be ready to talk with rangers and other visitors about the wonders of Denali National Park. Some of the words you'll want are listed here.

Alaska Talk

adaptation	adjusting or changing, in order to survive
alpine	above tree line
antlers	pair of branched bony, hornlike growths shed each year by animals of the deer family
arctic	area around the north pole
Athapascan	group of Alaskan Indian tribes
avalanche	large mass of snow, ice, or rock that falls suddenly down a slope
axis	straight line around which something rotates—The earth spins on its axis.
backcountry permit	free registration and permission to camp in the wilderness of the park
bull	male caribou or moose
burrow	hole in the ground made by an animal for its home
calf	young of caribou or moose
cheechako	one who has never spent a winter in Alaska; a newcomer to Alaska
crevasse	deep crack in a glacier; also crevice
cub	young of bear
cow	female moose or caribou

Denali	Athapascan name for Mount McKinley, meaning the high or great one	minimum impact	with the least possible force against— Minimum impact camping leaves hardly even footprints.
dog team	group of dogs used to pull a sled	mountaineering	art or sport of climbing mountains
dogsled	a sled pulled by dogs, used for winter transportation in some parts of Alaska	orbit	path of one body around another; the earth's path as it revolves around the sun in one year
ecology	study of living things and how they relate to each other and to their surroundings, or environment	outside	Alaskan term for anyplace outside of Alaska
ecosystem	the way all living things live together in an area	permafrost	permanently frozen ground
		plant community	type of vegetation well suited to an area
Eskimo	group of peoples of northern Canada, Greenland, and Alaska	predator	animal that kills other animals for food
ewe	female sheep	preserve	natural area where limited hunting is allowed
food chain	plants and animals in a community such as a forest where some animals eat plants and are eaten by larger animals that are eaten by other animals	prey	animal that is hunted and eaten by a predator
		protective coloration	skin or fur color that makes an animal hard to see
gee	command for dog team to turn right	ptarmigan	bird with feathered feet in the grouse family—Willow ptarmigan is Alaska's state bird.
gravel bar	strands of gravel piled up between parts of a river		
harem	a group of females that mate with one male	ram	male sheep
		refuge	area where animals are protected
harness	straps worn by sled dog—The harness makes it possible to hook the dog team to a sled.	reproduce	in plants, to produce seeds from which new plants can grow; in animals, to mate and produce young
haw	command for dog team to turn left		
hemisphere	half of a ball or sphere; in geography, the northern, southern, eastern, or western half of the earth	sourdough	Alaskan old-timer
		sow	female bear
		subarctic	region south of the arctic
		taiga	Russian word meaning ''land of little sticks;'' a forest where trees are not very tall
hibernate	to become inactive or dormant during a time when it's too cold for an animal to live normally		
hike	command to dog team meaning ''go''	Traleika, Trolika	high mountain; other Indian names for Mount McKinley
		tree line	point above which trees do not grow
horns	pair of permanent bony parts that grow out of an animal's head—Horns are permanent, but antlers are shed once a year.	tundra	Russian word meaning ''land of no trees;'' area above tree line where hardy, miniature plants survive in a very cold climate
husky	heavy-coated dog used in a team to pull a dogsled	tussock	clump of grass
		ungulate	hoofed animal
ice age	time in the past when part of the earth was covered with snow and ice for thousands of years	velvet	soft, fuzzy skin on antlers
		vole	small rodent the size of a mouse

Daylight at Midnight

Denali National Park is in the subarctic. This is an area south of the Arctic Circle, which surrounds the north pole. These regions get very little sun for most of the year. But in summer, there's daylight at midnight. Here's why.

If the earth were spinning on a stick, the stick would be tilted as the earth follows its orbit around the sun each year. The northern part of the earth is tilted toward the sun in summer and away from the sun in winter. In the spring, the northern half, the northern hemisphere, gets more and more sunlight each day. On June 21, the amount of sunlight in the north is the greatest. Sunset at Denali is at about 11:30 p.m., and the sun comes up again about an hour later.

On December 21, the earth is at a point in orbit where the "stick," or axis, tilts away from the sun the most. On this day, the sun rises around 9:30 a.m. and sets at 3:00 p.m. In some areas, there may be daylight, but no direct sunlight.

The warm growing season in Alaska is short, but plants get many hours of sunlight each day. During the winter, there's so little sun that the ground stays cold, very cold.

Summer Snow In The Subarctic

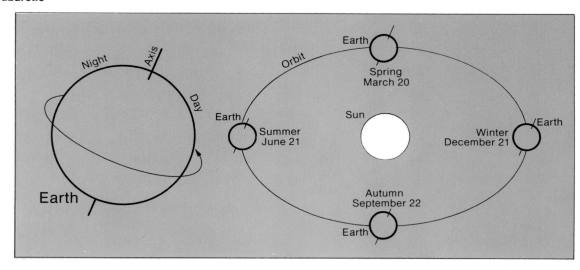

Night
Axis
Orbit
Earth
Spring
March 20
Day
Earth
Summer
June 21
Sun
Earth
Winter
December 21
Earth
Autumn
September 22
Earth

Glaciers

A million years ago, it was even colder in the subarctic, and the whole earth began to cool. For thousands of years during the ice age, much of North America was covered with ice hundreds of meters thick. Huge chunks of ice called glaciers moved slowly down the mountainsides. They gouged great hollows in the rock, carved peaks, and widened canyons.

When the ice age ended, many glaciers melted. But quite a few remain today on the frozen slopes of Alaska's mountains.

Moving glaciers pick up gravel, boulders, and other debris. This debris drops to the sides or rides along until it's dumped at the foot of the mountain. Piles and ridges of debris left by glaciers are called moraines.

Today many giant glaciers continue to grind their way down the sides of Mount McKinley, especially on the south. But a very long, famous one, Muldrow Glacier, begins near the highest peaks and reaches north almost to the park road. You have to look hard to discover the lower part of Muldrow because it's covered with gravel, soil, and plants.

Traleika Glacier

North End of Muldrow Glacier

Mount McKinley

Everyone goes to Denali National Park to see wildlife and the great Mount McKinley. This tremendous mountain was named in honor of the governor of Ohio who later became the 25th president of the United States.

Long before American explorers came here, Alaskan Indians called this mountain *Traleika,* high mountain, and *Denali,* the great one. Whatever you call it, this is the highest mountain in the United States. It has defeated many climbers. While summer can be warm at the top, temperatures can fall to well below 0° F, even in July. Temperature changes, high altitude, crevasses, and avalanches make Mount McKinley one of the most dangerous summits climbers have ever challenged.

For a long time, no one knew the true height of Mount McKinley or that the south peak is higher than the north one. Many people tried to climb it and failed. Finally a group called the Sourdoughs reached the top of the north peak in 1910. Three years later, an Alaskan, Walter Harper, was the first person to stand atop the higher south peak of the great one, Denali.

Adaptation

At Denali you'll discover how life goes on and on, sometimes under what seem to be the worst possible conditions. Living things adapt. They adjust to climate and soil by evolving, or changing.

How does a plant or animal "know" the changes it must make? It doesn't. But a plant that adjusts, or adapts, survives long enough to reproduce. Plants that don't adapt well die before they reproduce. This is called natural selection or adaptation.

White and black spruce trees have adapted to grow in the lowlands of the park. They grow in a forest called taiga, a Russian word meaning "land of little sticks." Among the spruce are other small trees: quaking aspen, white birch, and balsam poplar.

In the taiga, a thin layer of soil and gravel covers the permafrost, or frozen ground. Spruce roots cannot go very deep because the permafrost is like ice. Instead, the roots reach out in all directions to soak up water and plant food, or nutrients.

In winter, taiga plants stop growing. They store food in their roots and "go to sleep" until spring.

ga

Taiga Trees Have Shallow Roots

Lupine On The Taiga Floor

Taiga Residents

At Denali National Park, you'll discover several different plant communities. Each one has its own residents which have adapted in different ways.

The snowshoe hare nibbles green plants in the taiga all summer. Its brown summer coat makes it hard to see among the bushes. In autumn, the hare sheds this brown fur and grows a warm white winter coat. Then it blends with the snow. Big furry hind feet allow the snowshoe hare to jump across the deep snow without breaking through.

This little animal with its white coat and "snowshoe" feet has adapted in other ways as well. It has learned to eat the bark of willow, birch, and aspen during winter. Mother hares produce several litters a year, and the young are born with warm fur coats. This means a greater number survive.

When you walk in the taiga, you may discover other residents. Look up into the small trees to see the red squirrel. Look down to find holes where other creatures live in burrows. Listen. Take a guided walk with a park ranger and learn how these taiga residents adapt to life in Alaska.

wshoe Hare

Red Squirrel

What Lives In This Burrow?

Moose

Another taiga animal is the moose. This big member of the deer family roams through the taiga and into another plant community, the wet or shrub tundra.

Tundra means land of no trees, but wet tundra has dwarf willow, birch, and aspen. In winter, moose feed on the twigs of these trees. In summer, they add herbs and grasslike plants called sedges to their diet.

Every spring, a bull moose begins to grow antlers on his head. Through the summer the antlers are covered with a soft, fuzzy skin called velvet. By autumn, his antlers are very big. The moose rubs the velvet off the antlers and starts fighting with other males to "win" a bunch of females, or cows. The strongest bulls collect a harem of cows for mating. Would you call this a form of adaptation to produce healthy calves?

These strong bulls will pass on their strength to the young they father. The following spring, each mated cow has one or two calves. Moose cows may look clumsy, but they are quick to use their sharp hooves against bears and sometimes humans who get too close to their young.

Bull Moose

Moose Cow

Calves

Wet or Shrub Tundra

At times, moose roam to higher ground at the edge of the taiga. Here fewer spruce trees grow among dwarf birch, willow, and other shrubs. But rarely do moose go above tree line, the point beyond which trees cannot grow.

Above tree line, the tundra begins. Several months out of the year, the subarctic is dark and cold. In a winter twilight, tundra plants stand like tiny gray skeletons bent low to hide from the wind.

As summer sun warms the shrub tundra, plants seem to burst with leaves, blossoms, and berries. Insects become active. Small rodents scurry around after their long winter ''sleep,'' or hibernation. And the long-tailed jaeger soars over the tundra, ready to dive on its prey of lemming, vole, mouse, or ground squirrel.

Autumn comes early to the tundra. Leaves are gold, red, and brown by the end of August. Most of the birds fly south. Rodents crawl deep into their burrows to hibernate or to live on the plant food they've stored for winter.

Shooting Star—Tundra Flower

Long-Tailed Jaeger

Arctic Ground Squirrels

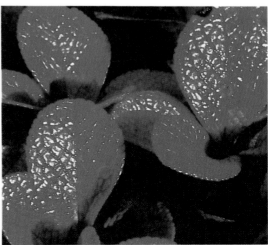

Bearberry Turns Red in Autumn

Tundra Birds

Among the bushy plants of the wet tundra, the willow ptarmigan waits through the winter. Its white winter feathers help it blend with the snow. Leg feathers cover even its toes and act as snowshoes that keep the bird from breaking through the icy crust. On winter's coldest days, this ground bird keeps warm in small hollows it makes in the snow.

In spring, the ptarmigan sheds its white feathers and becomes a brown speckled bird. Now it blends with the plants. If this protective coloration works, a passing fox won't see the bird hidden in tundra shrubs. Perhaps you'll discover other Denali creatures with this same kind of adaptation.

A willow ptarmigan makes its nest on the ground in June and lays 4 to 15 eggs. Once a mother ptarmigan begins to set, she seldom leaves her nest, except when the male does the setting. For 26 days they share the work of keeping the eggs warm until the chicks hatch.

Other birds commonly seen are marsh hawks, short-eared owls, sparrows, and mew gulls.

Willow Ptarmigan—Alaska State Bird

Mew Gull

Caribou

At Denali, you'll discover an animal that has made amazing adaptations to life in the arctic and subarctic. Caribou have developed special ways to survive in extreme cold.

This cousin of the reindeer is kept warm by fine fur and long, hollow guard hairs that keep its body warm. Large round hooves make it easier to trudge across the crusted snow or dig through it for food.

The caribou eats lichens. This plant can grow in poor soil and the harshest climate. Caribou have adapted to a diet of this low-protein food on which other hoofed animals could never survive. At the same time, a caribou can adapt to other foods when there are no lichens.

Migration is another form of adaptation. Caribou may spend the winter in the taiga, away from the screaming winds of the tundra. But in spring, they move on. By the thousands, caribou move to high ground to give birth to their young. Why do you think caribou have their calves in such cold, barren places where few other animals can survive?

Caribou Bull ▶

The Fight for Life

As soon as it's born, a caribou calf can stand and nurse from its mother. After one hour, a newborn calf is ready to travel if necessary. In two or three days, it can run faster than a person. A caribou grows fast, and by the end of August, the young animal is ready to leave its mother.

But death stalks all caribou, even though they have adapted well. Moving in huge herds that often stampede, a very young calf may lose its mother. Unless the cow finds her young, the calf starves.

Wolves often follow the caribou, watching for stragglers. Galloping across clumps of grass called tussocks, a calf can usually outrun a wolf. But sometimes a pack of wolves surrounds a tired old caribou or lost calf. Outside the park, caribou may face human hunters.

These animals probably suffer most during the summer. Sucking insects drain almost one liter of blood from each caribou every week. This cuts down on the energy both cows and bulls need to grow antlers and thick winter coats. To escape blood-sucking insects, some head for high, windy ridges when they've finished grazing the lowlands.

Caribou Cow and Calf

Caribou Yearling

Dall Sheep

When you see park visitors staring up at the high ridges, they're probably looking for Dall sheep. When it's munching on grass and herbs of the dry tundra, a sheep looks like a small patch of snow. But when a speck of white way up there moves, you know you're looking at a wild white sheep.

In a way, you can thank the Dall sheep and other animals for this national park. In 1906, Charles Sheldon came to the region to study Dall sheep. His feeling for the wildlife and scenery here caused him to start a movement to set the area aside as a national park.

Dall sheep are smaller than their Rocky Mountain cousins, the bighorn sheep. Rams (males) and ewes (females) both have horns. The ewe's horns extend back in gentle curves. A full-grown ram's horns are curled outward into a full circle. Sheep horns grow during the summer when food is plentiful and rich. Each winter, a ridge forms around the horn.

If you could get close enough to count the ridges on a sheep's horns, you would know its age. Otherwise, you can just guess its age and admire the Dall sheep from the warm shuttle bus.

Dall Sheep Ram ▶

Sheep Adaptation

On a Discovery Hike or in a program with a park naturalist, you learn how Dall sheep have adapted to the dry tundra high in the mountains. Coats of coarse, hollow hair and curly fur keep them warm. They have very strong legs that carry them swiftly up steep ridges, away from predators with less climbing skill.

Dall sheep spend their winters on high ridges where the wind blows snow off the grass they need to eat. In November or December, the rams begin to joust. When two rams want to mate with the same ewe, they stand several meters apart, then run toward each other and crash their heads together. After a few bashes, one of the rams walks away, leaving the "winner" to mate with the ewe. Ewes have their lambs about six months after they mate.

Late in spring, Dall sheep look down on the lowlands, searching for grizzlies and wolves. When their fine eyesight tells them it's quite safe, they cross the low country and climb to their summer feeding grounds.

When there are too many sheep, some of them must graze on lower hills where it's easier for wolves to catch a lamb or a weak old adult.

Dall Sheep Lamb

Moss Campion—Dry Tundra Plant

Two Kinds Of Fur Keep Dall Sheep Warm

Grizzly Bears

Grizzly bears survive by wandering and eating whatever food they find. When they come out of their winter dens, they often feast on carrion, the remains of animals that have died during the winter. Carrion also includes what's left after another animal has killed a Dall lamb or caribou calf.

Long claws on the grizzly's paws make it a good digger. Holes in the tundra may mean a bear has been digging for roots or into a squirrel's burrow.

Bears mate in spring or early summer, and a sow (female) has one to three cubs in the winter den. Each cub weighs less than two pounds and nurses from its mother. Cubs stay with their mothers through two summers. Then the sow chases them away, mates, and has more cubs.

Some say you might meet a grizzly bear anywhere in Alaska. A sow with cubs is very dangerous. Grizzlies have poor eyesight but good hearing and a good sense of smell. Take a tip from the Dall sheep and look carefully at any area you plan to hike. Scan the tundra or gravel bar with your binoculars. Then, to avoid surprising a bear, make noise as you hike.

Grizzly Bear

Grizzly Sow And Yearling Cubs

Wolves

Wolves are protected in this national park, but even so, they have learned to stay away from people. You may have to be content to see only the footprint of a wolf.

In a wolf pack, there may be a mother, a father, and other adult wolves. Four to six pups are born to the mother early in May. She stays with the young while the male goes out to hunt. When the pups are old enough, she may leave them in the care of another adult wolf and join the hunt.

To survive in the wild, wolves must be predators. They can get along for awhile by eating mice and ground squirrels. But ungulates, or hoofed animals, provide their main source of food. In spring, a wolf may chase a caribou herd and often catches up with a slower, weaker calf. During winter, old and sick animals fall prey to the wolf.

Some say the wolf keeps moose, caribou, and Dall sheep herds from getting too big. And, of course, only the swift and strong, the fittest ungulates, survive.

Gray Wolf ▶

Predator and Prey

It may seem cruel for a soft, fuzzy lamb, a moose calf, or a weak old caribou to become a meat eater's dinner. But wolves, foxes, and bears have eaten other animals since long before people were here to worry about death.

Each animal is a link in a food chain that begins when small animals like arctic ground squirrels and mice eat plants. These plant eaters, as well as moose, caribou, and Dall sheep, are called primary consumers. They are important links in the food chain, because they convert plants into the meat of their own bodies. They become the food supply for secondary consumers, the meat eaters.

Without predators to kill other animals for food, there would be too many hares, moose, caribou, voles, and sheep. The taiga and tundra would be over browsed and overgrazed. Many plant eaters would die of starvation. Then many predators would also starve.

In a national park, people try not to interfere with the age-old balance between predator and prey.

Caribou—Predator Or Prey ?

d Fox—Predator Or Prey ?

e—Predator Or Prey ?

Human—Predator Or Prey ?

People Adapt

During the ice age, a belt of land linked Russia with Alaska. Across that land bridge, the first people came to North America about 20,000 years ago. Perhaps they followed herds of caribou and moose. We know they hunted the now-extinct hairy mammoth.

These early hunters wandered over much of North America. Those that remained in the north were the ancestors of the Eskimo and Athapascan Indians.

Each group of people adapted. People who lived by the sea fished and hunted whales and seals. Inland groups camped on caribou migration routes. They lived mainly on meat that was rich in fat to keep their bodies warm.

The Alaskan Eskimo did not live in ice houses, but built one-room homes from wood, earth, and sod. The nomads, or wandering hunters, carried skin tents for shelter.

Animal skins were made into shoes called mukluks and hooded coats known as parkas. From birchwood and leather, early people made snowshoes that kept them from sinking into deep snow. They used the same materials to build sleds, then trained dogs to pull them.

wshoes

Ulu Knives For Skinning

Leather For Artwork As Well As Clothing

Dog Power

In Denali National Park, scientists search for the few places where early people may have camped. Even today, methods used by these ancient hunters help us adapt to Alaskan winters. Parkas and snowshoes made of modern materials make it possible for rangers to walk across deep snow in bitter cold. And dogsleds still provide one of the best ways to travel around the park.

When you go to Denali, you can visit the kennels where the sled dogs live in log doghouses. You get to pet the dogs before the ranger calls everyone together for a demonstration. He or she tells the history of dogsledding and shows how a sled works. And while there is usually no snow, wheels on the sled make it possible for the dogs to do what they like best.

Five to nine dogs pull a sled. The lead dog knows that "Hike!" means GO. When the driver yells "Gee!," the lead dog turns right. "Haw!" means turn left, and you know what "Whoa!" means.

Behind the lead dog are two swing dogs that help steer. The strongest dogs are back next to the sled in wheel position.

Today, dog power provides the best winter transportation at Denali.

g Doghouse

Sled Dog

Dogsled Demonstration

Denali and You

On a trip to this national park, you may discover that you, too, adapt. Quickly, you learn to prepare for all kinds of weather. Your legs get stronger from climbing ridges to see Dall sheep. Your eyes become sharper from searching for wildlife. Alertness keeps you aware and ready for a chance meeting with a grizzly bear.

Your adaptation may mean you adjust gladly to park rules that insure the protection of wildlife. You'll be happy that millions of visitors aren't jumping out of thousands of cars to take pictures of moose and caribou. If they were, most of the animals would hide in the backcountry where few could see them.

Park people hope you'll enjoy your park gently, with minimum impact. Let your hiking boots pick their way carefully across the tundra where plants struggle to survive. Clean up your campsite so even the mew gulls and eagles won't know you were there.

When you leave, take only memories of this vast wilderness. And may one of those memories be the sight of huge, ice-covered Mount McKinley in Denali National Park and Preserve.

Will The Eagle Know You Were Here? ▶

Alaska's Wilderness

Some say that before 1978, the National Park Service was missing the "crown jewels" of American parklands. In 1978, President Carter proclaimed 17 new national monuments in Alaska. In addition, about 100 million acres of public land were set aside by the Secretary of the Interior. An area almost as big as the state of California was to be studied so people could decide if and how this wilderness would be preserved for the future.

In 1980, Congress passed a bill that changed the name of the park from Mount McKinley to Denali National Park and Preserve. The bill also set aside many millions of acres for national parks, monuments, forests, and other public areas. Among them are volcanoes, glaciers, fjords, sand dunes, arctic tundra, wild and scenic rivers, rugged mountain ranges, and wildlife preserves and refuges. The "crown jewels" will be preserved for all people for all time.

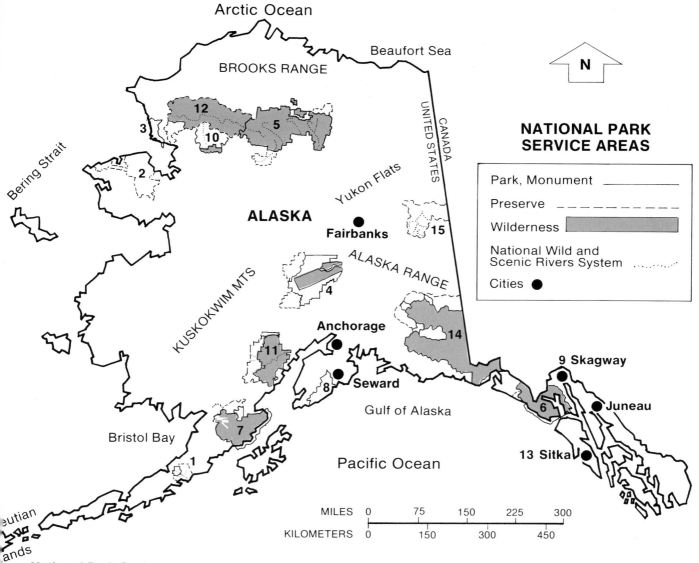

Arctic Ocean

Beaufort Sea

BROOKS RANGE

UNITED STATES / CANADA

Bering Strait

ALASKA

Yukon Flats

Fairbanks

ALASKA RANGE

KUSKOKWIM MTS

Anchorage

Seward

Gulf of Alaska

Bristol Bay

Pacific Ocean

Aleutian Islands

NATIONAL PARK SERVICE AREAS

Park, Monument	——————
Preserve	– – – – –
Wilderness	▓▓▓▓▓
National Wild and Scenic Rivers System	··········
Cities	●

9 Skagway
Juneau
6
13 Sitka

MILES 0   75   150   225   300
KILOMETERS 0   150   300   450

National Park System

1. Aniakchak National Monument and Preserve
2. Bering Land Bridge National Preserve
3. Cape Krusenstern National Monument
4. Denali National Park and Preserve
5. Gates of the Arctic National Park and Preserve
6. Glacier Bay National Park and Preserve
7. Katmai National Park and Preserve
8. Kenai Fjords National Park

9. Klondike Gold Rush National Historical Park
10. Kobuk Valley National Park
11. Lake Clark National Park and Preserve
12. Noatak National Preserve
13. Sitka National Historical Park
14. Wrangell-Saint Elias National Park and Preserve
15. Yukon-Charley Rivers National Preserve

Author and Illustrators

In writing books about the national parks, Wyoming-born Ruth Radlauer has seen summer snow in Alaska and snorkeled in warm winter waters of the Virgin Islands. From Maine to Hawaii and Washington to Florida, she has discovered the natural treasures of the United States as preserved in its national parks.

Graduates of the University of California at Los Angeles, Ed and Ruth Radlauer are authors of over 200 books for young people. Along with their adult daughter and sons, they photograph and write about a wide variety of subjects ranging from dolls to drag racing.

The Radlauers live in California where Ruth and Ed spend much of their time in the mountains near Los Angeles.

* * *

Born and educated in Massachusetts, Rick McIntrye now spends his *winters* at Death Valley National Monument in the California Desert where he works as a seasonal naturalist with the National Park Service. During the *summer,* he works at Alaska's Denali National Park and Preserve.

Rick's job at Denali gives him many opportunities to watch and photograph such animals as grizzlies, wolves, moose, Dall sheep, and caribou. His wildlife photographs have appeared in several books and magazines.